The Spirit Of Christmas

Calligraphy by
Joanne Fink

Great Quotations
Publishing Company

Calligraphy by Joanne Fink

Cover Design by Design Dynamics

Published by Great Quotations, Inc.

Library of Congress Catalog Card Number: 99-071626

ISBN: 1-56245-376-9

Printed in Hong Kong

This book is
dedicated to
everyone who
carries the
Spirit of
Christmas
in their hearts.

calligraphy by
Joanne Fink

JC1

The Christmas Season

IS ONLY AS MEANINGFUL AS WE MAKE IT

Christmas

IS NOT A SEASON.

IT IS A WAY OF LIFE.

May the
WONDERS
& JOYS OF
CHRISTMAS
be yours
to share with
those you
Love

Christmas;
awake,
salute the
happy morn,
whereon the
Savior of the
world was
born!

Christmas

consists of

OLD FASHIONED PLEASURES

HAPPY MEMORIES

& FAMILY TRADITIONS

The world
is filled
with the
Sounds of
Christmas
when you
open your heart
to hear them.

The best
YULETIDE
DECORATION
is being
wreathed in
smiles

JC8

It is good to
be children
sometimes,
and never
better than at
CHRISTMAS.

CHARLES DICKENS

CHRISTMAS

IS
TOO LARGE
TO BE
TUCKED AWAY
IN THE TOE
OF A CHILD'S
STOCKING.

JC10

*Who has not
loved a
little child,
he knows
not
Christmas
Day.*

JC11

When we throw out
THE
CHRISTMAS
TREE
we should be
very careful
not to throw out
the Christmas
Spirit
with it.

JC12

Christmas is many things

PEACE,

JOY &

LOVING;

FRIENDS,

FAMILY

& SHARING;

but it is the emotions

Christmas inspires

that makes us want

to keep Christmas

in our hearts

all year long.

'Tis the season
to be kindling
the fire of hospitality
in the hall, &
the genial fire
of CHARITY
in the heart.

Washington Irving

The spirit of
Christmas
brings Peace
& Happiness
to the
New Year!

JC15

No act of

Kindness

no matter

how small

is ever

wasted!

Aesop

I WILL
HONOR
CHRISTMAS
IN MY
HEART, AND
TRY TO
KEEP IT ALL
THE YEAR!

CHARLES DICKENS

At
Christmas
play & make
good cheer.

For Christmas
comes but once
a year!

AT

Christmas

ALL PEOPLE

SMILE IN

THE SAME

LANGUAGE.

You CAN
GIVE
WITHOUT
LOVING
BUT YOU
CAN NEVER
LOVE
WITHOUT
GIVING.

Every good gift & every perfect gift IS FROM ABOVE

JC21

*Blessed are those
who can give
without remembering
and take
without forgetting.*

*It is one of the most
beautiful compensations
of this life that no man
can sincerely try to
help another without
helping himself.*

Ralph Waldo Emerson

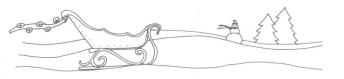

JC23

THE BEST THINGS TO GIVE

To your enemy -
  FORGIVENESS

To your opponent -
  TOLERANCE

To your friend -
  YOUR HEART

To your child -
  A GOOD EXAMPLE

To your parents -
  CONDUCT THAT WILL
  MAKE THEM PROUD

To yourself -
  RESPECT

To all people
  CHARITY.

JC24

THERE ARE LOYAL HEARTS

THERE ARE SPIRITS BRAVE

THERE ARE SOULS THAT

ARE PURE AND TRUE, THEN

GIVE TO THE WORLD

THE BEST YOU HAVE

AND THE BEST WILL

COME BACK TO YOU.

MADELINE BRIDGES

JC25

*Give
what
you
have*

TO SOMEONE.
IT MAY BE
BETTER THAN
YOU DARE TO
THINK!

Henry Wadsworth Longfellow

GOD'S *
GIFTS
*
*

put man's
best dreams
to shame.

*

*

JC27

NOTHING MULTIPLIES SO MUCH AS KINDNESS.

THE ONLY
TRUE
GIFT
IS A
PORTION OF
YOURSELF.

Gifts
can be found
on the seashore,
created out of
scraps, or
baked in the oven,
as long as
they are made
with Love.

JC30

YOUR
MERRY
CHRISTMAS

MAY DEPEND
UPON WHAT
OTHERS DO
FOR YOU,
BUT YOUR

HAPPY
NEW YEAR

DEPENDS UPON
WHAT YOU DO
FOR OTHERS.

Don't crowd
CHRISTMAS
into a
single day
but spread
its kindness
and humanity
throughout
the year

There is
no beauty
as great
as beauty
shared.

THE HEART
OF THE
GIVER
makes the
gift dear
and precious

MARTIN LUTHER

May we
be blessed
with
PEACE
in our time.

JC35

LET ALL
THE EARTH
CRY OUT
TO THE
LORD
WITH

Joy

PSALM 66

Love & Joy

at Christmas
can last
all year
long

REAL JOY

comes not from
ease or riches or from
the praise of men,
but from doing
something worthwhile.

WILFRED T. GRENFELL

JC38

One of the sanest, surest and most generous joys of life comes from being happy over the good fortunes of others.

ARCHIBALD RUTLEDGE

MAY THE
SPECIAL
JOY OF
CHRISTMAS
REMAIN
WITH YOU
THROUGHOUT A
BLESSED
AND HAPPY
NEW YEAR

PEACE

IS THE
EVENING
STAR
OF THE SOUL
AS VIRTUE IS
ITS SUN; AND
TWO ARE
NEVER FAR
APART.

COLTON

HOME
is the warmth
of loving hearts,
the light
from happy eyes,
kindness,
loyalty and
comradeship

Joy comes
not to him
who seeks it
for himself,
but to him
who seeks it for
other people

H.W. SYLVESTER

JC43

THE JOY OF
Christmas
IS A LASTING
TREASURE

JC44

WHEREVER
YOU ARE
it is your
own friends &
who make
your world!

WILLIAM JAMES

Not only at
CHRISTMAS
but all the year
through
the joy that you
give to others
is the joy that
comes back
to you!

May the
SPIRIT
OF PEACE
find its way
into each
moment
at Christmas.

JC47

*May all
the days of*
Christmas
bring you
JOY!

When you
really want
Love
you will
find it waiting
for you.

Love
is the
fairest flower
that blooms
in God's
garden.

Love IS SHARING A PART OF YOURSELF WITH OTHERS!

JANET HOFFBERG

THE
MIRACLE

OF
CHRISTMAS
IS THE
GIFT OF
Love

JC52

Love IS THAT
CONDITION
IN WHICH THE
HAPPINESS OF
ANOTHER PERSON
IS ESSENTIAL
TO YOUR OWN.

ROBERT HEINLEIN

Love
is the
ENCHANTED
DAWN
of every heart!

IT IS IN LOVING
not in being loved,
the heart is blest;

IT IS IN GIVING
not in seeking gifts,
we are at our best!

When
LOVE
adorns
a home
other
ornaments
are
secondary
matter.

After the verb
'TO LOVE'

'TO HELP'
is the most
beautiful verb
in the world.

BERTHA VON
SUTTNER

JC57

Above all
Love
is the gift of
yourself.

HAPPY
HOLIDAYS
To You

Blessed
is the season
which engages
the whole
world in a
Spirit of Love

JC59

*Never
forget*
THAT
THE MOST
POWERFUL
FORCE ON
EARTH IS
Love.

THE GREAT ACTS OF Love

are done
by those who
habitually
perform small
acts of kindness.

JC61

LOVE DOES NOT CONSIST OF GAZING AT EACH OTHER BUT IN LOOKING OUTWARD TOGETHER IN THE SAME DIRECTION

ANTOINE DE SAINT

FRIENDSHIP

IS ONE OF

THE NICEST

KINDS OF

Love

JC63

A friend is a present you give yourself.

ROBERT LOUIS STEVENSON

JC64

Share
your
JOY
if you wish
to have
more!

JC65

SINCE I HAVE
  NO GOLD TO GIVE
AND LOVE ALONE
  MUST MAKE AMENDS
MY ONLY PRAYER
IS WHILE I LIVE

GOD MAKE ME WORTHY OF MY FRIENDS.

JC66

WE SHOULD
BEHAVE
TO OUR
FRIENDS
AS WE WISH
OUR FRIENDS
TO BEHAVE
TO US!

ARISTOTLE

True friends
ARE LIKE
DIAMONDS
PRECIOUS
BUT RARE.

FRIENDS
are like flowers.
They bring joy
just by being.

JOANNE FINK

THERE ARE THOSE who pass like ships in the night. Who meet for a moment, then sail out of sight with never a backward glance of regret; folks we know briefly then quickly forget.

THEN THERE ARE FRIENDS who sail together through quiet waters and stormy weather helping each other through joy and strife. And they are the kind who give meaning to life.

Now may the warming love
of friends surround you
as you go down the path
of light and laughter
where the happy memories grow.

Helen Lowrie Marshall

Blessed are those

IT INVOLVES MANY THINGS

who have the gift

BUT ABOVE ALL THE POWER

of making friends

OF GOING OUT OF ONESELF AND

for it is one of

APPRECIATING WHATEVER IS

God's best gifts.

NOBLE & LOVING IN ANOTHER

THOMAS HUGHES

JC72

The best
way to
have a
FRIEND
is to be one.

A friend

IS SOMEONE
WHO HEARS
THE MELODY
IN YOUR HEART
AND HELPS
YOU SING IT!

JC74

A friend
IS SOMEONE
WHO NOT ONLY
ACCEPTS YOU FOR
WHAT YOU ARE
BUT MAKES YOU
FEEL GOOD ABOUT
BEING YOURSELF.

JOANNE FINK

JC75

MANY
PATHS
CROSS
AGAIN AT
CHRISTMAS

A Special Message:

_____

_____

_____

_____

_____

_____

_____

_____

_____

_____

_____

Other Titles by Great Quotations, Inc

Hard Covers

Ancient Echoes	Keys to Achieving Your Goals
African American Excellence	Lasting Impressions
Attitudes of Success	My Dear Mom
Behold the Golfer	My Husband, My Love
Celebrating Friendship	Never Ever Give Up
Commanders In Chief	The Passion of Chocolate
Dare to Dream	Peace Be With You
The Essence of Music	The Perfect Brew
First Ladies	The Power of Inspiration
Graduation	Seeds of Inspiration
Golf	Seeds of Knowledge
Good Lies for Ladies	Sharing Our Love
Heartfelt Affection	Sharing the Season
Improving With Age	Smile Now
Inspirations for Success	The Spirit of Christmas
Inspired Thoughts	Teddy Bears
I Thought of You Today	There's No Place Like Home
Journey to Success	Thoughts From Great Women
Just Between Friends	

Great Quotations, Inc.
1967 Quincy Court
Glendale Heights, IL 60139 USA
Phone: 630-582-2800 Fax: 630-582-2813
http://www. greatquotations.com

Other Titles by Great Quotations, Inc

Paperbacks

301 Ways to Stay Young

ABC's of Parenting

African American Wisdom

Angel-grams

A Servant's Heart

Astrology for Cats

Astrology for Dogs

A Teacher is Better Than Two Books

Birthday Astrologer

Can We Talk

Chocoholic Reasonettes

Cornerstones of Success

Daddy & Me

Erasing My Sanity

Graduation is Just the Beginning

Grandma I Love You

Happiness is Found Along the Way

Hooked on Golf

Ignorance is Bliss

I'm Not Over the Hill

In Celebration of Women

Inspirations

Interior Design for Idiots

Life's Lessons

Looking for Mr. Right

Midwest Wisdom

Mommy & Me

Mother, I Love You

Motivating Quotes

Mrs. Murphy's Laws

Mrs. Webster's Dictionary

Only A Sister

Parenting 101

Pink Power

Romantic Rhapsody

Social Disgraces

Stress or Sanity

Teenage of Insanity

The Be-Attitudes

The Mother Load

The Other Species

The Secret Language of Men

The Secret Language of Women

The Secrets in Your Name

Touch of Friendship

Wedding Wonders

Words From the Coach

Great Quotations, Inc.
1967 Quincy Court
Glendale Heights, IL 60139 USA
Phone: 630-582-2800 Fax: 630-582-2813
http://www. greatquotations.com

Other Titles by Great Quotations, Inc

Mini Calendars

365 Reasons to Eat Chocolate

All Star Quotes

Always Remember Who Loves You

The Candy Counter

Coffee Breaks

The Dog Ate My Car Keys

The Essence of Great Women

Extraordinary Leaders

Generations

Good Living

Heart Strings

Home Sweet Home

The Honey Jar

How to Speak Fluent Child

I Think My Teacher Sleeps at School

I'm a Little Stressed Right Now

A Kiss of Sun

My Friend & Me

Never Never Give Up

Older than Dirt

Shopoholic

Sweet Dreams

Talking To Men (and other dumb ideas)

Teacher Zone

Tee Times

A Touch of Kindness

Winning Words